A is for...
The Financial ABC's

Written by
Denae & Dean Chambers

ASSETS

Stocks & Shares

Insurance Policies

What you have

LIABILITIES

Credit Card

Student Loans

MORTGAGE
LOAN

BANK OTHER LOANS

What you owe

Illustrated by
Sameer Kassar

Instagram: @deanthewealthcoach

DEDICATION

This book is dedicated to my children. You are amazing, resilient and intelligent. I know you will change the world! I love you!

Hey Shiloh, I want to teach you about money using the alphabet.
Okay Denae.

B is for **budget**. A budget is a plan that helps us keep track of our money.

Budget

Income Expense

D is for...

DINOSAUR! ROARRR! I'M A T-REX!

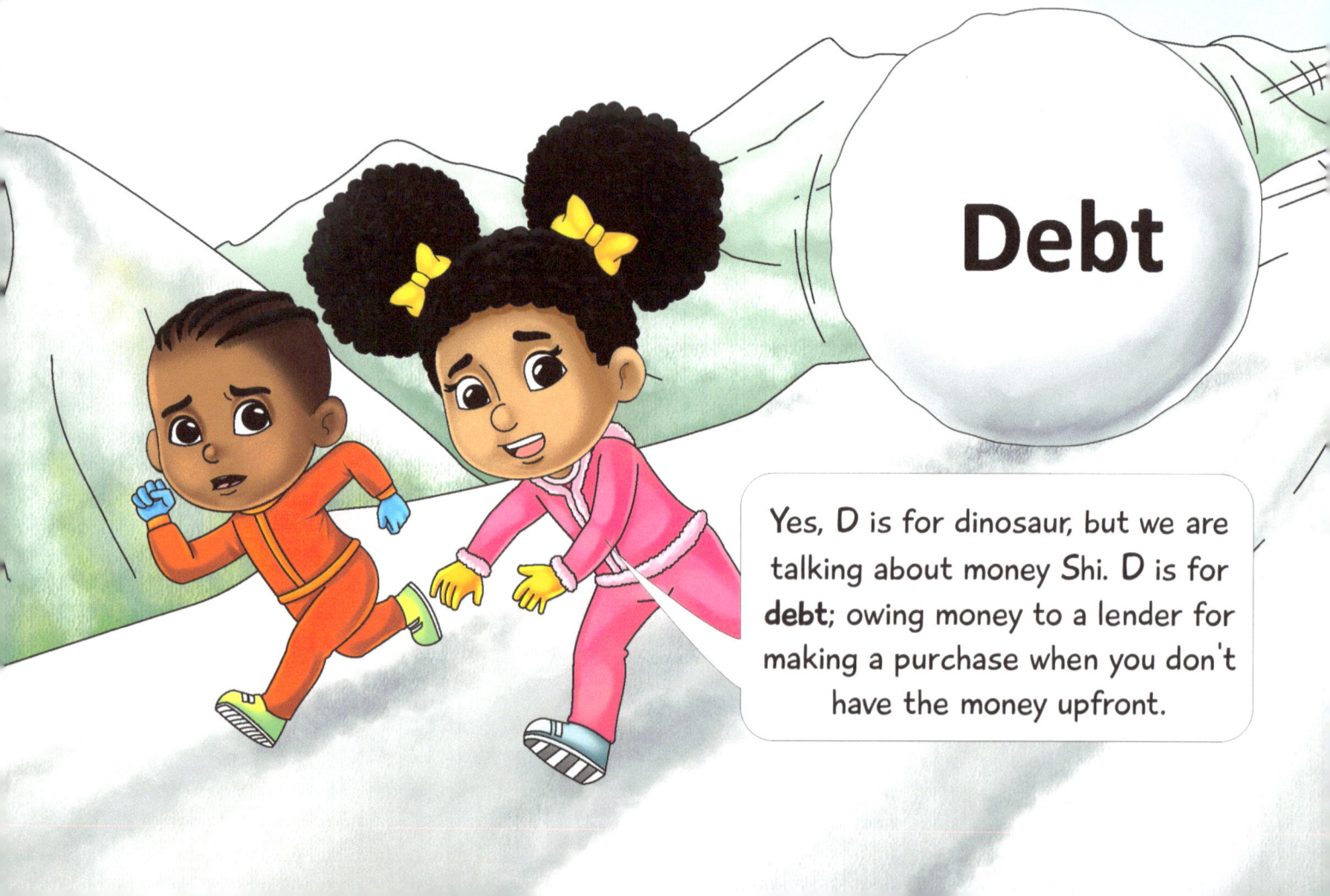

Debt

Yes, D is for dinosaur, but we are talking about money Shi. D is for **debt**; owing money to a lender for making a purchase when you don't have the money upfront.

E is for **emergency fund.** An emergency fund is money you put aside and save for when something unexpected happens.

F is for **financial literacy.** Financial literacy is understanding how money works. Our parents teach us about it every single day.

Assets ≷ Liabilities

Networth

G is for **gross income.** Gross income is how much money you make before any taxes are taken out.

J is for **job.** A job is something you agree to do in exchange for money.

N is for **needs**. Needs are important things we cannot live without, like food, clothes and shelter (a house).

O is for **overdraft**. It's when you spend more money than what you have in your bank account. Try not to use it.

P is for **profit**. That's how much money we would have leftover once we take away what we spent.

Income
-
Expenses
=Profit

Q is for **quote.** A quote is a price you give someone for a job that they would like you to do.

R is for R.O.I... That's....
Daaaad, what does R.O.I.
stand for again?
RETURN ON INVESTMENT.
THANKS! That's how
much money we make
on top of the amount
of money we invest.

S is for **saving.** Saving means to keep a portion of money that you get and not touch it! What's the first rule about saving Shi?
Always pay yourself first.
Awww, you're such a smart little boy.

U is for **unsecured loan.** This is when you borrow money without giving up anything (collateral).

Y is for...
Yellow!
Shiii! Fine, Y is for yellow. Aaahh! Actually, Y is for **yield,** which means income you gain on an investment.

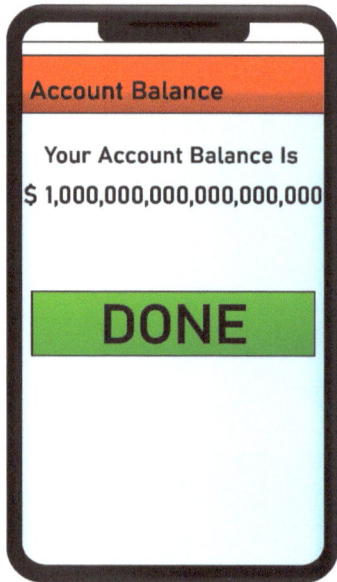

And that's the end. What did you learn Shi?
I'm hungry, can I have a bear paw?

www.ingramcontent.com/pod-product-compliance
Lightning Source LLC
LaVergne TN
LVHW072121070426

835511LV00002B/49